PROS AND CONS

THE DEBATE ABOUT SCHOOL
UNIFORMS

by Rachel Seigel

FOCUS
READERS

FOCUS READERS

www.focusreaders.com

Focus Readers is distributed by North Star Editions:
sales@northstareditions.com | 888-417-0195

Produced for Focus Readers by Red Line Editorial.

Photographs ©: ferrantraite/iStockphoto, cover, 1; AP Images, 4–5; xavierarnau/iStockphoto, 7; sirtravelalot/Shutterstock Images, 8–9; DGLimages/Shutterstock Images, 10, 23, 44; Red Line Editorial, 12, 34; RichVintage/iStockphoto, 14–15; Daisy Daisy/Shutterstock Images, 17; RossHelen/Shutterstock Images, 19; kickimages/iStockphoto, 20–21; Sascha Burkard/Shutterstock Images, 25; monkeybusinessimages/iStockphoto, 26–27; golero/iStockphoto, 29, 45; Fotos593/Shutterstock Images, 30; omgimages/iStockphoto, 32–33; antoniodiaz/Shutterstock Images, 36; mamahoohooba/iStockphoto, 38–39; asiseeit/iStockphoto, 41; Monkey Business Images/Shutterstock Images, 42

ISBN
978-1-63517-525-7 (hardcover)
978-1-63517-597-4 (paperback)
978-1-63517-741-1 (ebook pdf)
978-1-63517-669-8 (hosted ebook)

Library of Congress Control Number: 2017948099

Printed in the United States of America
Mankato, MN
April, 2019

ABOUT THE AUTHOR

Rachel Seigel is a longtime children's bookseller and reviewer who has spent more than 17 years working with parents, teachers, and librarians to match books to readers. She currently lives in Toronto, Ontario, with her boyfriend and her very large dog. She is the author of three other nonfiction books for children.

TABLE OF CONTENTS

CHAPTER 1

A HISTORY OF SCHOOL UNIFORMS

The modern school uniform dates back to the 1500s. A school in England required poorer students to wear blue cloaks and yellow stockings. These uniforms distinguished the lower classes from the rest of British society. As time went on, however, uniforms became popular with **prestigious** schools and the upper classes. Until 1972, Eton College in England was famous for its black top hats and tailcoats.

Many elite students attended Eton College, such as Prince Alexander of Yugoslavia (left) in 1937.

Historically, uniforms were most common in private and religious schools. But in 1987, Cherry Hill Public School in Maryland became the first US public school to have a uniform policy. By 2014, approximately 20 percent of US public schools required uniforms.

Typical boys' uniforms include dark pants, a light-colored shirt, a tie, and a jacket. Girls' uniforms are usually made up of a skirt or pants,

➤ UNIFORMS IN JAPAN

School uniforms in Japan started as a way to demonstrate the respectability of Japanese citizens. Girls' uniforms were modeled after the uniforms of the Royal Navy in the United Kingdom. Boys' uniforms were modeled after army uniforms. Today, the uniforms are a famous symbol of Japanese culture. They are especially popular in comic books and animation.

Some schools require two uniforms. One is for regular classes, and one is for gym class.

a tie, a blouse, and a blazer. Some schools have dress codes instead of uniforms. Dress codes ban certain items of clothing, such as short skirts.

Supporters of uniforms say that uniforms help improve students' performance in school. Uniforms create equality among students and can even make school safer. However, opponents believe uniforms take away students' individuality. They argue that uniforms are expensive for families and uncomfortable to wear.

CHAPTER 2

PRO
UNIFORMS IMPROVE SCHOOL PERFORMANCE

When students worry about their clothes, they are less able to focus on schoolwork. Many educators argue that revealing outfits and expensive clothing interrupt learning. Messages on clothing can also distract students. Uniforms remove these distractions. When students dress alike, they can focus less on what others are wearing. As a result, school becomes a better place for learning.

Science classrooms may have extra dress requirements, such as closed-toe shoes.

◣ Some schools require teachers to follow a dress code or uniform policy along with the students.

Uniforms benefit students' education by setting a more serious tone in school. The formal appearance of uniforms suggests that the school has a high academic standard. Therefore, students are more serious about their education. Uniforms change how others **perceive** students as well. Research shows that teachers view students in uniform as having a more positive attitude.

Students in uniform are also more likely to follow school rules. In one survey, 85 percent of principals reported that uniforms increased classroom discipline. Putting on a uniform every day gives students a sense of discipline. It may also help students learn respect for authority. Uniforms distinguish students from those who are in charge at school. This improves relationships between teachers and students.

DID YOU KNOW? ◄

When students in Kenya started wearing uniforms, they attended school more often and behaved better. The uniforms made school seem more important to students and families.

Uniforms can also improve school attendance. Students who wear a uniform don't need to pick out an outfit in the morning. And they have fewer fights with their parents about clothing choices. This helps them get to class on time. In four Cleveland area public schools, attendance

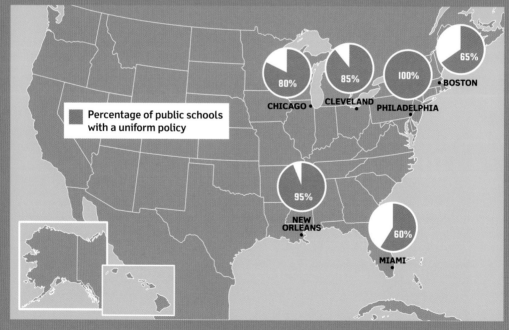

US CITIES WITH HIGHEST USE OF PUBLIC SCHOOL UNIFORMS

Percentage of public schools with a uniform policy

CHICAGO 80%
CLEVELAND 85%
PHILADELPHIA 100%
BOSTON 65%
NEW ORLEANS 95%
MIAMI 60%

increased by 3.5 percent when students switched to uniforms.

Other studies show that students in uniforms pay more attention in class. They also participate more in class. Attendance and participation affect students' class grades. Some schools that require uniforms even have higher graduation rates than schools that don't.

Not all students have good judgment about clothing. Uniforms teach students that an **appropriate** outfit is based on more than personal preference. Uniforms also prepare students for their futures. Many jobs have a dress code or a uniform. If students wear uniforms at school, it will be easier for them to follow dress codes at work. By wearing a uniform, students learn how to dress appropriately. They learn that what they wear matters in society.

CHAPTER 3

PRO
UNIFORMS BUILD STRONG SCHOOL COMMUNITIES

Schools are more than places for learning. They are also complex social environments. Students face constant judgment at school. When their peers like them, students feel happy. But sometimes, students don't feel liked. Judgment from their peers makes them feel left out. This has a negative effect on their attitudes toward school. Unhappy students may want to drop out.

Like sports teams, many schools use uniforms to promote teamwork and community.

At their best, schools are communities that give students a sense of belonging. Uniforms help create this community. By wearing the same uniform as others, students feel like they belong to a close group. The community becomes part of a student's **identity**. Uniforms also promote teamwork and school spirit. When students wear uniforms, they take pride in their school.

Without uniforms, students feel pressured to fit in. Students often judge one another on their clothing. This can lead to the formation of **cliques**. A student might become popular for wearing expensive or trendy items. However, many students come from families that can't afford expensive or new clothing. If students don't keep up with clothing trends, they may feel embarrassed. They may also be teased or bullied. These students might not want to go to school.

⚠ Bullying isn't always physical. Gossip can be a form of bullying, too.

Statistics show that 90 percent of students in grades four through eight report being bullied. And an estimated 160,000 students miss school every day due to bullying. Removing the pressure to dress a certain way helps students feel equal.

In many cases, students feel relieved when they wear uniforms. When students stop treating school like a fashion show, they feel less afraid of rejection. They are treated more equally, and their self-esteem improves.

All students have the right to learn without the fear of being judged. Uniforms send students the message that everyone is welcome. When students wear uniforms, others get to know them by their character, personality, and schoolwork—not by their clothes. Students learn that who they are is more important than what they wear. This

> ## ➤ DID YOU KNOW?

The students at Chicago's Urban Prep Academy use their uniforms as a form of motivation. When seniors are accepted into college, they exchange their red ties for red-and-gold-striped ties.

▲ Students can express their skills and interests through hobbies, such as art.

allows them to express themselves in ways other than how they dress. Some may choose to express themselves through school activities or clubs.

CHAPTER 4

PRO
UNIFORMS MAKE SCHOOLS SAFER

In the last few decades, reports of crime at school have increased. In the United States, for example, approximately 3 million students experience crime at school every year. As a result, school security is an important concern for both students and teachers.

Studies show that uniforms reduce **harassment** and crime in schools. Personal attacks are less likely to occur when students wear uniforms.

Uniform policies prevent students from storing valuable clothes and accessories in their lockers.

There are also fewer conflicts over who has more money or the better clothes. By keeping expensive clothing and jewelry at home, students are less at risk of being robbed. Uniforms also prevent students from hiding weapons underneath baggy clothing. This makes violent crimes harder to commit.

When students are all dressed alike, it's easy to spot someone who doesn't belong in the school. This allows teachers to easily identify intruders who want to cause harm or disruption. Strangers are less likely to enter the school if they know they will stand out.

Uniforms are also helpful in reducing gang activity in schools. Members of the same gang usually wear a specific color or style of clothing. Their clothes may also contain a symbol that represents the gang. By wearing a uniform,

▲ Uniforms make it difficult for strangers to blend in with students.

students in gangs cannot wear the gang's colors or logos. This makes it harder for gangs to **recruit** new members. When gangs are less visible in school, students feel safer and less intimidated.

School uniforms keep students safe outside of school as well. When students are on a field trip, teachers can recognize the students from their school. If a student gets lost or separated from the group, it's easier to find him or her. If students leave school without permission, they can be identified by their uniforms. Uniforms also identify students as youth. Students can't pretend to be older than they are. This can prevent them

> ## UNIFORMS FIGHT VIOLENCE

In 1994, Long Beach Unified School District in California adopted a school uniform policy. The district hoped the policy would fight growing rates of school violence and gang activity. After one year, reports of assault with a deadly weapon decreased by 50 percent. Reports of fighting, robbery, and drug possession also went down.

⚠ Schools have strict rules against possession of weapons and drugs.

from getting into dangerous situations, such as

buying alcohol or cigarettes.

CHAPTER 5

CON
UNIFORMS LIMIT FREEDOM OF EXPRESSION

Clothing is an important part of how people express themselves. Color, fabric, and style choices show off an individual's personality. Many opponents of school uniforms worry that uniforms threaten self-expression. They say that forcing students to dress alike takes away their individuality.

Students often wear T-shirts that have funny messages, band names, or sports logos on them.

Most students feel more comfortable in the clothes they pick out themselves than in uniforms.

These features allow students to express their personalities. Schools have often banned T-shirts with political or social messages. Many people think this violates students' freedom of expression. In most cases, courts have agreed. Students should be able to wear what they want, as long as the clothing is appropriate. Outfits must not promote illegal activity.

By limiting students' freedom of expression, uniforms promote **conformity**. They send a message to the school and community that students are all the same. Schools should instead encourage diversity and choice. Diversity teaches students that everyone is different. And despite differences, everyone deserves respect. Choosing between options teaches students to make good decisions. Forcing students to wear uniforms limits both diversity and choice.

Students who dislike how their clothing looks may have difficulty focusing on school.

Students begin to express their individuality when they are young. They also start having opinions about their bodies. These opinions may be positive or negative. Allowing students to wear what they want means they can choose clothing that makes them feel good about themselves. This promotes positive **self-image**. If students dislike their clothes, they might also have negative feelings toward their bodies.

▲ Many Muslim students wear a hijab, which means "cover" in Arabic.

Some uniform policies **discriminate** against students of certain cultures and religions. For example, some schools try to prevent gang activity by banning baggy pants, scarves, and bandanas. But these items could be part of a student's culture. Some cultural hairstyles, such as box braids, are also banned in some schools.

In other cases, students have been banned from wearing religious **attire**. Many religions have required ways of dressing. School uniforms can force students to choose between their uniforms and their faith. Some schools make exceptions to their policies to avoid this problem. However, this creates another issue. A student might be bullied if he or she is the only one not wearing a uniform.

STANDING UP TO RELIGIOUS DISCRIMINATION ◁

In 2007, a 14-year-old student spent nine weeks in school suspension for wearing a metal bangle to school. The bangle, known as a kara, is an important symbol of the Sikh faith. But the school refused to make an exception to its policy against jewelry. The student and her family took the school to court. A judge ruled that the school was guilty of discrimination.

CHAPTER 6

CON
UNIFORMS DON'T FIX REAL SCHOOL PROBLEMS

Many educators argue that uniform policies do not fix the real problems in schools. One of the largest of these problems is bullying. Some educators may hope that uniforms will solve bullying. But students will always be different from one another. They can be picked on for their gender, religion, grades, likes, dislikes, and more. Attempting to remove students' differences will not end bullying. It may even make bullying worse.

Students find many ways to bully one another, including online and over text messages.

When students appear to be the same, they are less accepting of diversity. This results in more bullying.

Uniforms do not eliminate gangs, either. Clothing is not the only way that gangs identify themselves. They may use hand signals,

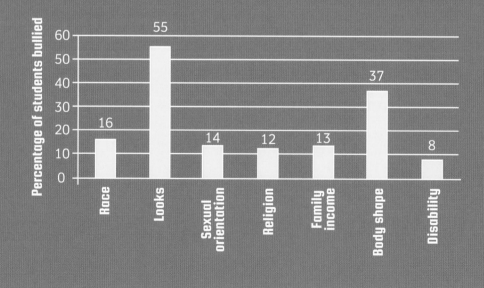

MOST COMMON REASONS STUDENTS ARE BULLIED

Percentage of students bullied

Race	16
Looks	55
Sexual orientation	14
Religion	12
Family income	13
Body shape	37
Disability	8

accessories, and tattoos instead. Uniforms also make it harder for teachers to identify gang members. When students are dressed the same, gang members can hide within the school. Uniforms only cover up gang problems in schools. They do not fix the wider problem of gang violence.

Uniforms can also lead to conflict between schools. Uniforms identify students as members of a particular school. This creates a divide between students from different schools. Students may view those from other schools as rivals. This can increase fights between students who attend different schools.

It takes more than uniforms to fight violence in schools. Schools must instead focus on changing the school environment. They can hold violence-prevention courses to educate students.

Many people argue that detention, especially for students who break uniform policies, does not serve a purpose.

Schools can also work with the police and encourage students to report crimes.

School uniforms do not fix education problems either. National studies on the effectiveness of school uniform policies show that uniforms do not increase students' motivation to learn. The same studies show that uniforms do not improve academic achievement. Students succeed when they have the support they need for learning. This is true whether students wear uniforms or not.

In reality, uniforms take time away from students' education. Teachers must make the time and effort to enforce uniform policies. Some students break the policy on purpose to get out of class. When students have to change or wait for parents to bring them new clothes, they lose class time. Sending kids home takes even more time away from school.

DID YOU KNOW? ◄

In September 2014, the Coseley School in England sent 100 students home on their first day for wearing the wrong shoes. The school uniform policy required black leather shoes.

CHAPTER 7

CON
UNIFORMS CAUSE GREATER INEQUALITY BETWEEN STUDENTS

Inequality occurs in schools when certain groups of students are treated unfairly. Supporters of school uniforms may argue that uniforms make students more equal. But many students, families, and teachers think school uniforms add to problems of inequality.

One example is economic inequality. Uniforms are an extra cost that many families cannot afford. Kids still need clothing to wear outside of school.

Some families spend more than $300 per child, per year, on school uniforms.

This means parents end up spending more money than they would if uniforms were not required. Replacing uniforms throughout the year also becomes expensive. Children grow quickly and can be rough with clothing. If the family is unable to replace the clothing, children must wear clothes that are torn or don't fit.

In families with more than one child in school, clothing and uniform costs are even higher. Families must also pay for other school costs, including supplies and lunch. On top of these costs, uniform policies can be unfair to lower-income families.

Uniforms do not hide income differences. In fact, some educators argue that uniforms single out low-income students. Approximately 47 percent of public schools in low-income, urban areas have uniform policies. This percentage

In 2014, the average cost of a school lunch in US middle schools was $2.37.

is much higher than the 6 percent in suburban neighborhoods. Within schools, students' personal items, such as smartphones or tablets, reveal students' economic background. Some students may use accessories or makeup that other students' families can't afford.

Uniforms may try to hide income differences, but they do not prevent inequality. Students still notice differences between their peers' wealth.

Some school uniform policies require girls to wear skirts year round, including in the winter.

And they are still able to judge one another based on these differences.

Gender inequality is another example of inequality in schools. Often times, there are more rules for girls' clothing than boys'. For example, many schools argue that girls' clothing distracts boys. Schools often ban certain items, such as short skirts and tank tops. These policies treat girls unfairly by holding them responsible for boys' behavior. As a result, boys do not learn respect or responsibility. Meanwhile, girls feel humiliated and ashamed.

Uniform policies with separate rules for boys and girls are also unfair to students with a different **gender identity**. Some students might not identify as either male or female. These students may prefer pants, dresses, or clothing that is gender neutral. Some students might identify as female but dislike dresses. Others might identify as male but prefer dresses. Uniform policies often require students to wear clothing they don't feel comfortable in.

DID YOU KNOW? ◁

Many private schools in the United Kingdom are changing their uniform policies to be gender neutral. In 2016, 80 UK schools allowed students to wear uniforms that were designed for the opposite gender.

PROS

- Uniforms set a more serious and academic tone in schools.
- Students in uniform pay more attention to schoolwork and less attention to their clothing choices.
- Uniforms create a sense of community in schools and promote school spirit.
- Uniforms create a more equal learning environment.
- Uniform policies can reduce crime, bullying, and harassment in schools.
- Outside of school, uniforms help teachers, families, and law enforcement identify missing students.

CONS

- Uniforms prevent self-expression and individuality in students.
- Some uniform policies lead to religious discrimination.
- Uniforms cannot make up for missing educational programs.
- Uniforms do not eliminate competition or bullying between students.
- Enforcing uniform policies takes time away from students' education.
- Many families cannot afford the cost of uniforms.
- Uniform policies are often biased against girls.

FOCUS ON
SCHOOL UNIFORMS

Write your answers on a separate piece of paper.

1. Write a paragraph that summarizes the pros of school uniforms outlined in Chapter 4.

2. Do you support school uniforms? Why or why not?

3. What percentage of suburban public schools have uniform policies?

   A. 6
   B. 90
   C. 47

4. Why do students targeted by bullying sometimes miss school?

   A. They are suspended.
   B. They cannot decide what to wear.
   C. They are afraid to go.

Answer key on page 48.

GLOSSARY

appropriate
Fitting for the situation.

attire
Formal clothes.

cliques
Small groups of people that are hard for others to join.

conformity
A change in behavior to fit into a group.

discriminate
To treat others unfairly because of who they are or how they look.

gender identity
A person's sense of being male, female, neither, or a blend of both.

harassment
Behavior that makes someone feel unsafe or uncomfortable.

identity
The traits, labels, and beliefs that people use to define themselves.

perceive
To view someone or something in a particular way.

prestigious
Highly respected or honored.

recruit
To seek out new members for a group or activity.

self-image
A person's view of his or her appearance.

TO LEARN MORE

BOOKS

Allman, Toney. *School Violence*. Chicago: Norwood House Press, 2017.

Bily, Cynthia A. *Dress Codes in Schools*. Detroit: Greenhaven Press, 2014.

Klein, Rebecca T. *Your Legal Rights in School*. New York: Rosen Publishing, 2015.

NOTE TO EDUCATORS

Visit **www.focusreaders.com** to find lesson plans, activities, links, and other resources related to this title.

INDEX

Answer Key: **1.** Answers will vary; **2.** Answers will vary; **3.** A; **4.** C